and a short history of the
Liège
TROLLEYBUS SYSTEMS

425 and a short history of the LiègeTrolleybus Systems

First Published 2005

ISBN: 0-9511013-2-3
EAN: 978-0-9511013-2-2

Printed and bound by Bakes and Lord, 529 Beacon Road, Bradford

Published by Bobtail Press, 22 Main St, Haworth, West Yorkshire BD22 8DA

This publication is copyright of R. S. Ledgard, 2004.

All rights reserved. Contents may not be reproduced in any form, except for short extracts for review, without the written consent of the publisher.

Acknowledgements

In producing the booklet, my thanks go especially to the following contributors for historical information and use of their photographs – a letter by their name corresponds to that found with the photographs.

Historical information was obtained from transport enthusiasts, employees and suppliers in the late 1960's, and presents a simplified account. For the 'rivet-counting' enthusiast, the recent publication 'Aux Fils des Trolleybus' is recommended.

A.	Louis Clessens of Liège	Edmond Robert of Liège
B.	Rene Hanssen of Liège	J H Renard of Jemeppe, Liège
C.	Sandra Ledgard of Bradford	British Leyland Archives
D.	Susan Tetley of Bradford	W J Carmen of Guernsey
K.	Ransomes, Sims and Jefferies, Ipswich/University of Reading Archives	
L.	Fabrique Nationale d'Armes de Guerre s.a. Archives	
M.	Société des Transports Intercommunaux de la Region Liégeois	
N.	Société Nationale des Chemins de Fer Vincinaux	

Other photos are by the author, or of unknown origin.

Especial thanks to Shirley Ledgard, for booklet layout, and for trying to make my free-hand diagrams presentable. And to Bakes and Lord (Printers) of Bradford for technical advice.

THE PRESERVATION OF LIÈGE 425

And this is how it happened ....

In the early 1960's trolleybus preservation was the buzz. John and I considered various vehicles – Hull, Bradford, Ashton, but a big problem (apart from finance) was where a double decker could be stored. On one of his business trips to Germany, John passed through Liège, Belgium and photographed one of the 'ancient' trolleys there (actually one of 1938 vintage). How about buying one of these? Big plus: A single decker!

Knowing nothing of the Liège system, we wrote to ask if there might be any serviceable vehicles being withdrawn soon, and how much. You might imagine our surprise when we received a reply from the General Manager saying that some vehicles were to be withdrawn soon, costing 15,000 Belgian Francs. Would we like one? That was all the information we had at the time, but casting all doubts aside we replied: "Yes please".

Somehow members of a British enthusiast group got to know of this intention and came to inform us that, as they were intending purchasing an English-built trolleybus from Liège, we'd be wasting our money. Nonplussed, and with joint contributions (15,000 Bf converted to £108) John and I had the purchase price, but there was the problem of transportation – a trolleybus is hardly the sort of thing to send by post! First we contacted the Automobile Association who initially advised a low loader, but eventually with persistence their Belgian colleagues were contacted and towing became the plan. Enter Alf, who offered a tow vehicle, a driver (himself) and a specially designed tow bar, for a very reasonable fee. Through him, Total (GB) Ltd provided the fuel for the truck in return for an advert on the trolleybus; and some support was obtained from Gannex (suppliers of PM Harold Wilson's raincoats).

Arrangements were only half completed when Liège wrote again, in December 1965, to say: "We've got a trolleybus for you. Come and get it!"

The prospect of a winter tow was ruled out, and Easter 1966 was decided upon, in the hope (ill-founded) of better weather.

With most things arranged, our group set out, John, Rod, Susan and myself by train, arriving in Liège and checking into an hotel just across from the main station – right on a tram and trolleybus route! Alf came over in his truck, taking 22½ hours for the 400 miles – not too bad with the roads as they were then.

The next couple of days we all went our ways to film, photograph and research the Liège system. We visited the STIL offices, and waved our wad of correspondence at the doorman. We were ushered across the impressive Est-Ouest Tramways insignia on the main entrance floor, up a majestic flight of stairs, along a polished wood floor corridor and into a spacious office panelled in light oak. The room was furnished with a substantial desk and an ample supply of comfortable chairs, and a carpet all suggesting a degree of luxury. Behind the desk was a well-dressed gentleman of ample proportions, completing the image of prosperity by puffing continuously on a large cigar. Compare this with the average English GM's office! Except this guy was 'only' the Chief Engineer! We were given a tour of the depot and in the yard shown the incomplete remains of an ancient trolleybus, which was being restored for a museum in Brussels. It wasn't like the one John had photographed. The CE laughed, saying that <u>those</u> were from 1936/38 and still had a few years to run. Our vehicle was 1932, the same as in the yard here. Horrified at the thought of acquiring a vehicle in kit form, we anxiously asked to be shown ours. Next day April 13th, we went to St Foy depot (which we had visited earlier looking for our vehicle). There, in the shadows of a shed, was our T32, number 425. The shedmen refitted the battery and other bits which had been removed when 425 was withdrawn; riveted on towing triangles and affixed our GB registration. 425 was run out into the almost deserted yard – dusty, dirty, but still complete! After filming a few runs in the yards, Alf arrived. He went to fit the towbar to the front axle – and managed to touch something he shouldn't, getting a mild shock in the process. Rod and the shedman lowered the trolleys. Good thinking!

425 awaiting departure from St Foy depot 13/4/66   D

425 was one of the last six T32's in service. Four were stripped for scrap. The fifth (432) was about to suffer the same fate when enthusiasts stepped in, and she was hurriedly being reassembled for preservation in Belgium (as we had seen at Cornillon). Hitched up, and ready to roll, John presented the STIL representatives with a copy of the Bradford Trolleybus Jubilee booklet.

The Tow begins! Leaving St. Foy, watched by locals from above and a shedman at the front. D

With their car they led us quietly out of St Foy, passing the remains of 404 – the English trolley which the British group were thinking of buying. Definitely a waste of money! Along the cobbled streets and along Rue Ste Walburge (passing the 23 terminus) and Chaussée de Tongres to the motorway, where they waved a fond farewell as we circled up the ramp, not just to us but also to 425, whose gong we clanged in acknowledgement. We had the impression that Liège loved its trolleybuses.

"If the hills around Liège were higher, we'd have hydro-electric power, and the trolleybuses would remain", commented an STIL official. "The rising cost of electricity is a main consideration in trolleybus abandonment."

The first few miles on the motorway were taken at a steady 30 mph. John was driving. Rod, Susan and myself were investigating, and finding how things worked inside. On the dashboard was a pressure gauge which was steadily creeping up – by trying various levers, we found that the vehicle's motion provided compressed air to operate the doors. Cash trays for driver (OMO) or conductor could be fitted, and the destination blinds were in good condition.

Some of the hard, leather covered seats were a bit tatty – and very uncomfortable on a long drive!

This was the original layout – but now the saloon seated 26 plus conductor, with a large platform inside the rear door – standing was 30 places. We used the platform for luggage, souvenirs (eg bus stops, and advertising plates which hung on the 'bonnet' doors) and for 'on board' catering. Tyre treads were good but one tyre wall had a slit. The ride was firm but the steering was heavy, being not power-assisted. Like all Liège trolleys, 425 had retrievers.

Two doors on the front of the vehicle gave access to the control equipment, both high and low voltage. (See previous picture.) Note the large white ceramic fuse on the right! The 6 bulbs in series steps the voltage down for a seventh bulb, which is the line power indicator. On the driver's side of the 'bonnet' is the series contactors, operated with the driver's left foot pedal; centre is the forward/ reverse/ regenerative braking contactors operated by lever; on the near side the drum parallel contactor, operated by the driver's right foot. The mechanical brake pedal is between the other two, right foot operated.

A view through the cab door of a T32 showing 3-pedal control. The skate switch is just visible on the extreme right. Levers are handbrake, reverser, door controls (2) and gong rod.   All photos courtesy of FN.

A Note on Trolleybus Skates

All pre-war trolleybuses had provision for a skate, known as 'un trainard'. This consisted of 3 steel blocks which could slide in grooved tramrail. The blocks were attached to each other and to the trolleybus chassis with a strong chain. At the left side of the driver was a changeover switch so that the negative (return) circuit could be either via trolley or skate.   Thus the vehicle could traverse tram routes where trolleybus wires were not provided.

The towbar proved most successful. We frequently clocked 50 mph on the motorway. There was a communicator wired between trolley and tow truck but also a signal for 'emergency' stop – "If I put my rear spotlights on", said Alf, "you walk on the brakes because my truck won't stop you".

We ran through the centre of Bruxelles, receiving a few curious stares, and arrived at Ostend in a total of 6 hours. We over-nighted in a B & B on the 'prom' in Ostend. Susan slaved over a hot stove on the rear platform making soup, and Rod improvised a destination blind: Liège-Huddersfield.

425 with Alf's tow truck at Ostende Ferry Terminal 13/4/66   M

April 14, and it began to snow. We headed down the coastal road, passing Vincinaux trams and miles of sand dunes heading for the ferry from Calais. Out of Belgium and into France in a howling blizzard. Dead stop. Although we'd been told that our papers were in order, the French would have none of it. In the way for which they are renowned, the Customs Officers refused to communicate in English. We tried our smattering of French. Nothing doing. They just turned their backs on us. In frustration we spontaneously saluted them in the manner popular in a neighbouring country some 20-odd years before, and stormed out of their scruffy little shed. This resulted in the guards ordering us, at pistol point, to turn round and leave France immediately.

Back to Ostend where we discovered there was a midnight ferry to Dover. When we'd first enquired (in GB) the fare for the vehicles had been quoted as £100 – twice as much as from Calais. Now we were told £30. Good news, but – Ooops – 425 exceeded the height limit, by about a foot. The trolley base was the problem. Now, unbeknown to us, Alf had worked on trolleybuses in

Huddersfield <u>and</u> he had a well-equipped tow truck. With the aid of a borrowed ladder Alf went atop. The base was lowered down on a rope – pretty heavy – and stowed inside together with one boom. The other boom was lashed on the roof. A multitude of ferry passengers and officials watched our performance. We felt like going round with the hat!

We were ready to drive on, with less than an hour to spare, when we had a visit from Customs. They had decided, now, that we needed an export document, which couldn't be obtained until the next day. Fortunately we'd struck up a good relationship with the AA and RAC representatives there and, after they argued our case with customs for 30 minutes, and a couple of trips by a Customs officer on his pedal bike, the matter was resolved. We carefully reversed onto the ferry.

Some newspapers had been forewarned of our venture, and although none made contact on the ferry (because we'd not caught <u>that</u> ferry), they did pick up on us when we arrived in Dover in the early morning of April 15. Most published rather 'fairy tale' accounts, being ignorant of what a trolleybus was, but some reported more accurately our opinions of the French.

However, a trolleybus was also an unusual import for Customs.

"What is it?"
"A trolleybus".
"Looks more like a tram. And it's being towed, so it must be a tramcar trailer. That'll be the least duty I can charge you."

Nice one, Customs!

425 awaiting departure from Welwyn Garden City 16/4/66   D

The weather had eased and we now laboured up the Canterbury road, through the Dartford Tunnel. Before we entered the attendant advised: "Get some speed up down the slope or you'll hold up the traffic on the uphill far end". That said, Alf proceeded to put it into practice. In the tunnel, two buses can pass safely if both keep well to their left. John's driving position was such that he could only see the kerb a few yards ahead. Sudden swerving would not be a good idea, so John just hung on to the wheel and hoped. Emerging from the tunnel was like ending a ghost train ride! Welwyn Garden City was reached for an overnight stay.

In the morning, we proceeded as far as the first of WGC's many roundabouts and ground to a halt. 425's handbrake was stuck (or frozen?) on. Alf got out and got under with a lump hammer and wrench, and we were away again.

We then continued up the A1. At some point for whatever reason, John decided to try the electric braking. Bang! The main switch above John's head cut out with a flash, and scorched the cab ceiling, doing John's nerves a lot of no good. It shouldn't have been on anyway. Alf calls: "You've got smoke coming from the roof!" In the snow and rain, the resistances on the roof had shorted and set the wooden framework smouldering. Fortunately it was soon extinguished. Onward through the snow to Alf's garage at Shepley where 425 stayed for some days while the local papers visited Alf, and until proper accommodation could be found for her. Our average speed Liège to Huddersfield worked out at just under 20 mph. Considering the legal maximum for towing in GB was 20 mph, we reckoned it a good performance. Over the next two months 425 was kept at warehouses in Cottingley and Keighley. A friendly forklift truck driver helped the trolleybase reassembly. On 3/8/66 425 moved to the former B & B bus garage in Bradford.

The burnt-out resistance on the roof had been wired across, and an array of traction batteries obtained from Newcastle at £6 per crate, so 425 could be moved under battery power around the sheds. But we wanted to run under wires!

John arranged for 425 to be tested at Thornbury Works, Bradford, on the 19th August. Huddersfield trolleyheads were fitted, in place of the short, carbonless Liège ones. Perhaps not surprisingly 425 was deemed unsuitable for the Bradford system because of her regenerative braking and an inadequate mechanical brake. Having driven cautiously out of the works, we were granted permission to drive up and down the yard <u>on the wires</u>! Running over tramlines may have brought back memories of 425's home town. 425 now moved to Frizinghall, where she was joined by Nottingham 506.

Being unable to run on the Bradford system, we opted for running by gravity and batteries, to be incorporated with the hire of a Bradford trolleybus for a tour of the system – a hire charge in those days of about £4.10s per 4 hours, plus an extra £1 if you wanted to visit Bowling Yard!

425 leaves Thornbury Works after brake testing   C

425 was joined at Frizinghall by Nottingham 506

We had discovered that the differential/back axle on 425 had been made by David Brown – a Huddersfield company. They were contacted and were very interested in our activities for inclusion in their house magazine.

425 was duly taxed for the road – a new number was allocated GKU 429E (for some technical reason) as from 10/2/67. Insurance was organised.

425 was towed to Chapel Lane, Allerton courtesy of David Browns

With a tour date arranged, David Browns were advised, and they suggested bringing over one of their tractors to do the towing. On the day, 506 was taken to Thornton Road, as a static exhibit. 425 was taken to Chapel Lane, on the Allerton route. With half of the tour party transferred from BCT to STIL at Chapel Lane (the others continuing the tour) we drove to City via Thornton Road where we met the tour trolley 835 again. 425 ran around the centre via Forster Square to Leeds Road and was towed empty to Laisterdyke to await the transfer of the other half of the tour party. All went well down Leeds Road until approaching the lights at the bottom of Harris Street. They were on red as we approached – and with a police car stopped there ahead of us! Now 425's mechanical brakes are really only for final stop. And traction batteries don't take kindly to regenerative braking. With a smell of hot brakes and potentially hot underpants we careered down Leeds Road. Fortune smiled on us – the lights changed and Noddy's pal drove off! 425 returned to Frizinghall.

But I really wanted to film 425 running with her trolleys on the wires. Bradford City Transport was contacted with a view to operation (sans regenerative braking) on various disused routes, or even the training yard. A polite "no", but the GM did say that Wakefield Road could not be used because the overhead had been dismantled. The plan was formed. 425 was insured for a day – about £3; two willing BCT trolleybus drivers, one in uniform, came along; a local garage towed 425 to the 'dismantled' Wakefield Road wires. Of course they were still there, live, for the driver training trolleys to get to and from Bowling training yard. 425 performed cautiously for filming, with the uniformed driver at the wheel. On arrival in City we were spotted by an inspector who must have reported the matter. Very soon I received a letter from the Town Clerk threatening dire consequences for trespass on Council wires which we'd been told weren't there! A few days later a circular arrived at depots to the effect that any non-Bradford trolleybus found using the system was to be apprehended and reported. A similar communiqué was issued for the final weekend of trolleybus operation in Bradford.

Prior to John and myself relinquishing our financial interest in 425, she appeared in a bus rally in Huddersfield, towed by a vintage ex-army 6-wheel wrecker from Quarmby, and in company with Huddersfield trolleybus 631 towed by a Bradford double-deck motorbus! 425 made a short journey on batteries through the assembled motorbuses. In 1995 there was a concern about 425's survival. News passed to enthusiasts in Belgium who began a campaign to repatriate her. She passed eventually to Sandtoft Trolleybus Museum near Doncaster. When funds and facilities were available, she was refurbished electrically and mechanically, although by this time certain parts (eg the reversing lever!) had disappeared. By 2003, 425 was fit to run on the Sandtoft circuit, performing as sprightly as ever.

'Neither flamboyant nor graceful, 425 has an endearing quality'.
A flashy youngster from Limoges blocks 425's progress. Sandtoft 2004.

Three other Liège trolleybuses are preserved in the Public Transport Museum in Liège: T32 432 in 1940 style; Type IV 544; LS 402 as original.

One gets away! 425 emerges from storage at St Foy. D

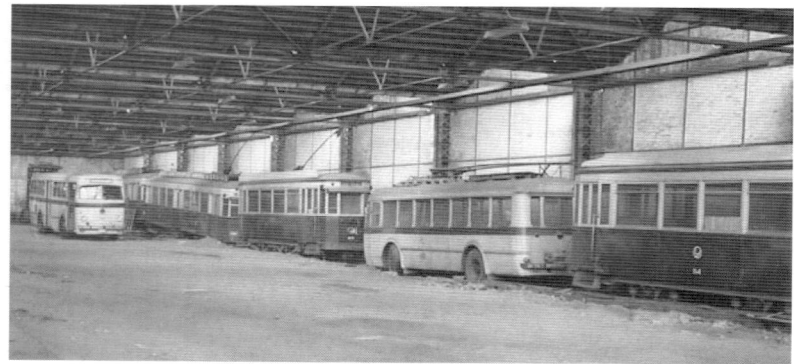

Others remain. T38 453, LS trams 114, 45, unknown, 321, motorbus 68. Motorbuses 61, 62 and tower wagon 5588.P were also there.

Not a good preservation venture! Ransomes 404 rotting away in St. Foy yard 1966   D

Alf's truck carefully tows 425 into the mill yard at Cottingley

425, now equipped with batteries, is tucked up with bales of wool in Wall's Shipping warehouse in Keighley

425 in Wakefield Road, Bradford as Stan films her progress.   C

425 runs along the tram lines in Thornbury Works Yard, maybe reminiscing about her companions the Liège trams, or maybe hoping she has a brighter future than BCT 27, awaiting scrapping.   C

425 has an impromptu race with a tower wagon, up Thornbury Works yard

425 passes under the railway bridge, Wakefield Road, Bradford

425 in Wakefield Road, Bradford. Driver Gordon Hyde poses as a confused would-be passenger. "Where's the door?"   C

425 approaching Bradford centre – City Hall is just around the corner!   C

LIÈGE – CENTRAL
Pre-Trolleybus Era

The town of Liège, situated just over 60 miles ESE of Bruxelles at the confluence of the rivers Meuse and Ourthe, was founded around 550 AD. In the time of Louis XI, in 1691, there occurred the Massacre of Liège when 40,000 persons were killed and the town was reduced to ruins. Re-building, and development of manufacturing, together with river transport, and later railways, saw Liège prosper. It became the centre of a coal mining area, and of engineering in the Herstal and Seraing areas. The inhabitants are of Walloon stock, speaking a dialect of French. Although in Belgium, many inhabitants considered themselves French. The town may be called Liège, Luik, or Lüttich. In August 1914, the commandant at Liège, General Leman, met the advancing German army. He was defeated but Liège was not destroyed. Likewise in WWII, damage was done to the environs, but wholesale destruction did not take place, although in 1940 the Belgian army destroyed all the bridges and the Germans intensively bombed the industries in 1944/45.

Liège had horse trams. Some were double-deck open top with two staircases and lettered 'Chemin de Fer Americain Liégeois'. Next came interurban steam trams of the LS, with electric traction from 1904.

The town of Liège was mainly served by Reseaux Liégeois et Est-Ouest Tramways. This company developed an extensive town network, becoming Société Anonyme des Tramways Unifies de Liège et extensions (TULE), then Société des Transports Intercommunaux de L'Agglomération Liégeoise (STIAL). Another company to operate into Liège was Société des Railways Economiques de Liège-Seraing (adding 'et Extensions' from 1925), known as the RELSE. It operated trams from Liège to Jemeppe from 1882. RELSE became Société des Transports Intercommunaux de Liège-Seraing (STILS). In 1964 STIAL and STILS merged to become Société des Transports Intercommunaux de La Région Liégeoise (STIL). Did you follow all that?!

For clarity, RELSE, often called just LS, ran services from Liège to and around Seraing. TULE ran services based in and around Liège and suburban routes, except for outlying private motorbus routes, and SNCV metre-gauge tramways which passed through Liège (terminus at Théâtre) as street tramways.

Until 1929, electric trams reigned supréme. At that time, track renewal was becoming urgent, and new regulations concerning highway maintenance were being introduced, together presenting tram operators with a considerable financial burden. For example, tram operators were being compelled to maintain a greater width of roadway along their tram routes. Although the tramways were administered by the TULE (an amalgamation of town council and private sector – the first of its kind in Belgium), the private secotr alone dealt with the finances. In Liège town it was decided to try out trolleybuses.

A route was created from Cathédrale up to the suburb of Cointe (Pl. du Batty). A fleet of 5 vehicles was ordered from Ransomes in England. They were shipped from Harwich to Zeebrugge in 1930. In a very short time the operators wrote to Ransomes expressing their appreciation of these vehicles and of the warm reception given them by the travelling public. Further new trolleybus routes and tramway conversions began almost immediately.

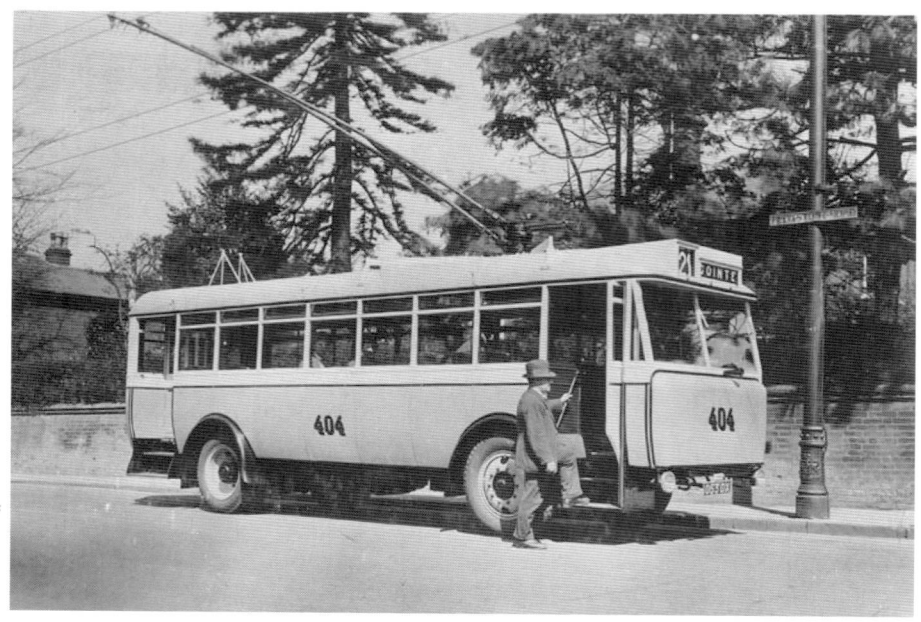

Liège 404, with Ransomes plates 053DX on test in Felixstowe Rd, Ipswich   K

The Trolleys Reign

1930 to 1940 saw new trolleybus routes and tramway conversions aplenty. New trolleybus routes 20-25 were created, and trolleybus routes 26-29, 31, 32 and 35 were, in essence, tramway conversions and the route was often extended, either to find space for a turning circle, or to better serve the expanding suburbs. In the town, the termini were Théâtre, Cathédrale or Pl. St. Lambert. Trolleybuses often shared town streets with trams. However, conversion of routes from tram to trolley also occurred where the two forms of transport used the same roads, once out of town. The concept of trolleybus feeders for tram routes (as briefly with Oupeye and Cheratte at Herstal) was unacceptable. In 1931 the tram fleet was about 200, trolleybuses 6 and motorbuses 3. By the late 1930's, trams were down to about 150, trolleys up to 90, and motorbuses down to 2.

Ransomes 405, as original, at Cointe 1930   B

Ransomes 401 in Rue de Sluse 1933   B

Ransomes 406 on R. St Gilles in 1933, with temporary tram-type route number   B

A tight squeeze for 419 and tram 49 in Rue St. Gilles, 1930's   L

Then came the War. The Belgian army blew up bridges over the Meuse, which put a stop to cross-river routes, but as there were depots on both sides of the river, services mostly continued.

432 at Renory terminus with bomb damage evident   B

German bombing caused widespread damage to the industrial areas along the Meuse, especially Ougrée, Renory and Herstal. Tram and trolley overhead was dismantled around Guillemins – thought to be a likely target for bombing. One account claims 5 trolleybuses were destroyed (see next paragraph): Another account claims none were, but several had to wait until 1947/48 for rebuilding.

The occupying forces, it is said, requisitioned T32's 407, 408, 409 and (possibly all) the Brossel trolleybuses of 1938, for service in Wilhelmshafen and maybe also Trier. Although they all returned, 495 and 496 were deemed unrepairable and scrapped, along with 407, 408, 409. Brossel 497 faired little better on its return – it was converted to a motorbus No. 35 (later becoming 82).

More serious than the interruptions in the power supply was an increasing shortage of tyres which crippled trolleybus services, so much so that by the end of the War only 7 vehicles were operational! Many services were suspended anyway from 1944 to 1945 to assist allied forces to take control. Within 3 months supplies enabled 50 vehicles to return to service – the British Army helped with 400 second-hand tyres!

Cornillon Depot 1943 with 493, 504, 505 awaiting repairs. B

In 1943, as soon as reconstruction of the Herstal area was finished, it was desired to extend tram route 5 beyond Herstal and to reintroduce tram 6 to Wandre. However the replacement bridge over the Meuse and the Albert Canal was not designed for tramlines. So trolleybus wiring was erected from Herstal (Place Licour) to Wandre then to Cheratte, and to Oupeye through Vivegnis, considerably extending both routes. A turning loop was provided at Wandre. The trolleys were extended in 1949 into Liège, to Cathédrale via Quai Ernest Solvay. The trams continued to run from Guillemins to Coronmeuse (1) until 1964, and St Lambert-Coronmeuse then R. Hayeneux to Herstal (5) until 1963.

Henne depot 1943, with 481, 440 and others in the shed, 446, 444, 456 and others in the yard, which was the way into the shed via a tight curve at the back. B

In 1952 a trolleybus was temporarily imported from the USA. This was from the Marmon-Herrington company, and was fitted with Westinghouse electrics. Number 1324, it was the last of a batch ordered by the Cleveland authority. During late 1951/early 1952 it toured Europe, being displayed at the Brussels Automobile Show. The Belgian company Ateliers Metallurgiques of Nivelles were interested in building under licence: They were a company said to have 'many ideas which usually came to nothing!' The vehicle was evaluated in Liège. It underwent testing mainly on the Oupeye and Trooz routes then it returned to the USA in 1952.

FN/ACEC Type IV at the FN factory 1954

As a result of this, a batch of new, high capacity trolleybuses was built in 1954-1956, by FN/ACEC, under licence. These were quite speedy vehicles. In 1956 the fastest timetabled route was trolleybus 37 Oupeye at 28 km/hr. The fastest motorbus route was 30 Embourg at just over 24 km/hr.

In 1956 there was considerable re-organisation of the power distribution system for trams and trolleys. Instead of the three substations on the town supply, the new Linalux generating station supplied 7 substations at Cornillon, Coronmeuse, Henne, Vivegnis, Grivegnée, Homvent and Ans. (Laveu remained supplied from the town generator). The final tram to trolleybus conversions occurred in 1956 with routes 10 and 12.

Despite all this, the flexibility of the motorbus was turning the TULE against electric traction. Most of the fleet was pre-War, and the infrastructure did not adapt well to the increasing traffic and re-organisation in Liège centre. In 1959 the TULE still had 3 active tram routes; 4 Circular Guillemins-St. Lambert-Vennes-Fragnée-Guillemins, 1 Guillemins-Coronmeuse, and 5 St. Lambert-Herstal, with 19 trolleybus routes, and half-a-dozen motorbus routes.

The Decline

By 1964, the changes were evident. Trolleybus routes 24, 37, 38, 26, 27, 28, 31, 32 had been converted to motorbus, with about half of the T32's, a third of the T36's, and the remaining Brossels and Ransomes having been scrapped. .

As trolleybus routes were closed the wiring was not always dismantled immediately. For example, for 6 years after the Trooz route closed, wiring was still in place along it from Pl. Barth. Vieillevoye (just clear of tram route 4) through to beyond Rue E. Vandervelde, except for the removal of the junction for Streupas at Pont des Grosses Battes and the junction for Embourg near Chenée Gare. A pair of disconnected parallel inward bound wires were also remaining from Pont des Grosses Battes to Boulevard de Douai.

Liège Central Area

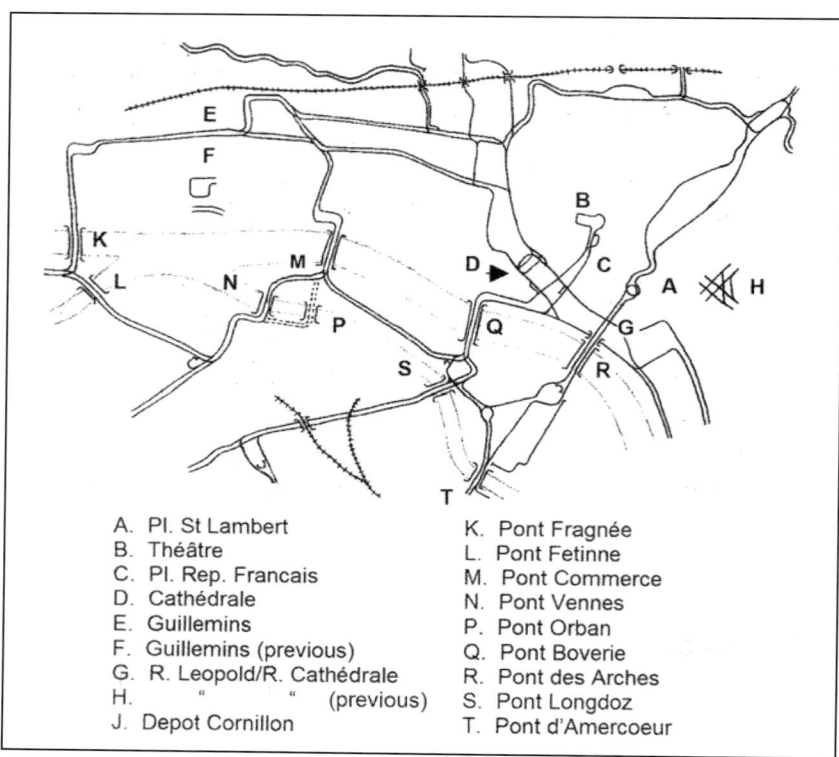

A. Pl. St Lambert
B. Théâtre
C. Pl. Rep. Francais
D. Cathédrale
E. Guillemins
F. Guillemins (previous)
G. R. Leopold/R. Cathédrale
H.   "   "   (previous)
J. Depot Cornillon
K. Pont Fragnée
L. Pont Fetinne
M. Pont Commerce
N. Pont Vennes
P. Pont Orban
Q. Pont Boverie
R. Pont des Arches
S. Pont Longdoz
T. Pont d'Amercoeur

This plan gives a general idea of the town termini, Pl. St. Lambert, Théâtre (and latterly Pl. de la Republique Francais), Cathédrale, and Guillemins. Apart from Guillemins, the termini changed little, but the routes through the town changed considerably over the years.

All electric traction ceased on 9/11/71.

Liège Trolleybus Routes

Route No.	To	Town Terminus	Open	Closed	Route Length (Km)	Ref
10	FLERON	St Lambert	1956	9/11/71	9.4	
11	BEYNE	St Lambert	1956	9/11/71	6.9	1
12	LONCIN	St Lambert	1956	9/11/71	6.1	
12 barré	ANS (Ste Marie)	St Lambert	1956	9/11/71	4.5	2
20	COINTE	Cathédrale	1/8/30	1969	3.1	
21	LAVEU	Cathédrale	1934	1969	3.7	
22	BURENVILLE	Cathédrale	1933	1969	3.4	
23	STE WALBURGE	Cathédrale	1939	1969	5.5	3
24	THIER Á LIÈGE	Cathédrale	1934	1964	5.2	
25	OUGREE (Beau Site)	Cathédrale	1935	1965	11.3	
26	STREUPAS	Théâtre	1937	1963	6.9	
27	RENORY	Théâtre	1937	1962	8.4	4
28	VENNES-STREUPAS	Théâtre	1937	1961	6.5	
29	THIER DE CHÊNÉE	Théâtre	1938	1969	6.0	
30	EMBOURG	Cathédrale	1943	1955	10.0	5
31	TROOZ	Théâtre	1937	5/12/61	13.9	
32	HENNE	Théâtre	1937	5/12/61	7.8	6
33	VAUX SOUS CHÈVREMONT	Théâtre	1937	1969	7.3	
35	ROBERMONT	Théâtre	1937	1969	4.4	
37	OUPEYE	Cathédrale	1949	08/01/65	11.1	7
38	CHERATTE	Cathédrale	1949	17/12/63	10.3	7

Notes

1. Effectively a short working of 10.
2. Effectively a short working of 12. Turning loop at Rue des Écoles, near Ans railway station.
3. A reverser at Pl. Ste Walburge was later replaced with a loop off the main road. Re-numbered 36.
4. Originally to a reversing triangle at the far end of Rue Renory. Later extended via R. de la République to Rue d'Ougrée, then along route 25 wires as far as R. de J. Wauters (Ougrée Gare). The section Kinkempois to R. de la République was abandoned. There was also a 'half reverser' at Rue Thiernesse. Here vehicles reversed up the slight incline, then free-wheeled out into the main road.
5. Trolleybus route Guillemins to Angleur Gare 1939/40. Re-introduced 1943 to a reverser at Embourg (Voie de Liège).
6. 32 was the replacement for tram 15 Henne, a short working of tram 14 Trooz, on the south side of the river Vesdre. However trams (15) continued to run to Chenée station until 20/1/38. 32 was extended from the original terminus Henne Viaduc to the 33 terminus and also called Vaux sous Chevremont. Viaduc loop was retained.
7. Herstal (Pl Licour) to Oupeye and to Cheratte commenced 1943.

The routes taken between town and terminus often varied over the years.

Liège Trolleybus Destination Blinds

Many variations may be found, for example Route 35 has GRIVEGNÉE instead of THÉÂTRE LONGDOZ; Route 21 has BD KLEYER instead of LAVEU. (Boulevarde Gustave Kleyer links both Laveu and Cointe termini – confusing!). 22 has ST NICOLAS instead of BURENVILLE, 25 has THIER À LIÈGE GUILLEMINS OUGREE between 36 and 27 with another 25 (as per list). Appearing between 12 and 20 is 12 barré ANS with ST LAMBERT additional. ANGLEUR is terminus Streupas.

Some earlier blinds had separate destinations for inward or outward service.

Short workings, possible on most routes, were not on the blinds.

Blinds carried a coloured background to the route number, according to the route corridor served. An all-red background was shown for SERVICE and for DEPOT CORNILLON.

A typical blind of the 1960's reads as follows:

NUMBER	MAIN DESTINATION	CITY & VIA
10	FLÉRON	ST LAMBERT
11	BEYNE	ST LAMBERT
12	ANS LONCIN	ST LAMBERT
20	COINTE	CATHÉDRALE
21	LAVEU	CATHÉDRALE
22	BURENVILLE	CATHÉDRALE
36	ST WALBURGE	CATHÉDRALE NANIOT
37	OUPEYE	LIÈGE HERSTAL
38	CHERATTE	LIÈGE HERSTAL
24	THIER À LIÈGE	CATHÉDRALE
25	OUGRÉE	CATHÉDRALE GUILLEMINS
	(Blank)	
26	ANGLEUR	THÉÂTRE FETINNE
27	OUGRÉE GARE	THÉÂTRE FETINNE
28	ANGLEUR	THÉÂTRE VENNES
30	EMBOURG	
31	TROOZ	THÉÂTRE CHENÉE
29	THIER-CHENÉE	THÉÂTRE LONGDOZ
32	HENNE	THÉÂTRE LONGDOZ
33	CHEVREMONT	THÉÂTRE LONGDOZ
35	ROBERMONT	THÉÂTRE LONGDOZ
	SERVICE	
	DEPOT CORNILLON	

Liège route plan at maximum

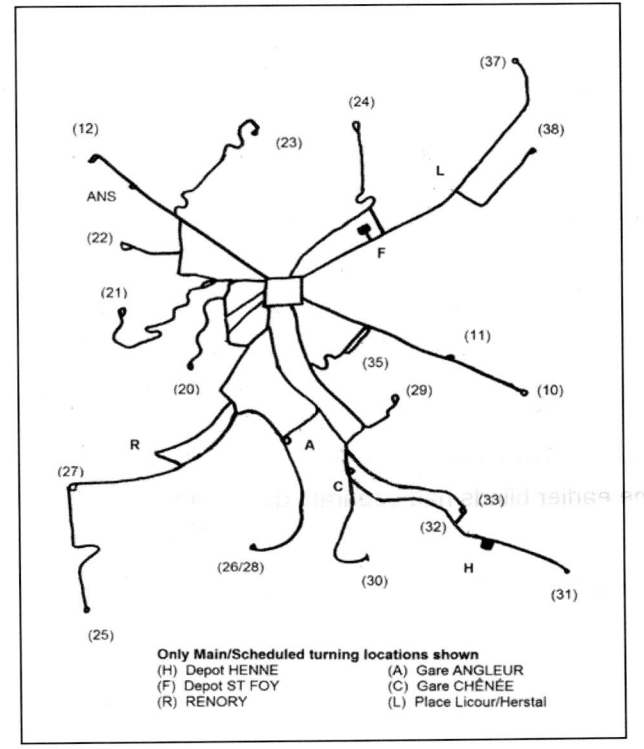

Only Main/Scheduled turning locations shown
(H) Depot HENNE (A) Gare ANGLEUR
(F) Depot ST FOY (C) Gare CHÊNÉE
(R) RENORY (L) Place Licour/Herstal

ROUTES TO THE SOUTH EAST

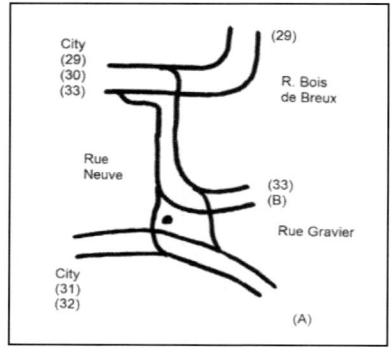
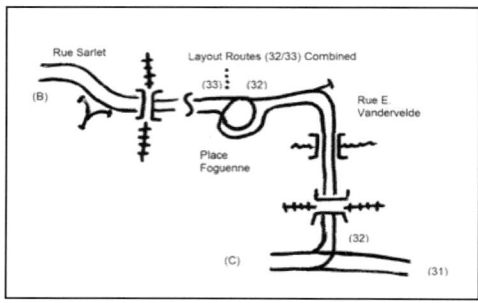

Brossel 500 turns at Chevremont on the opening (26/6/50) of the shared terminus of routes 32 and 33. A tower wagon is standing by, just in case of problems! B

Route 33 turned at Pl. Foguenne. Route 32 at a loop at Henne (Viaduc), just East of Chenée station. In 1939 32 was extended to the 33 terminus, the routes being 33 Béchuron-Vaux-Henne (clockwise) and 32 (anti-clockwise). In 1950, they reverted to two separate routes, turning at Vaux. 32 closed, together with 31, in December 1961.

In the event of a problem at Pl. Foguenne (e.g. parades or flooding!) 33 turned at the reverser at Pl. Balthasart/Rue Sarlet. 32 reversed into the stub near Pl. Foguenne and fly shunted out. Although the loop was simplified after 1962, the stub and 32 trailing frog remained – utterly useless – until 1969.

ROBERMONT

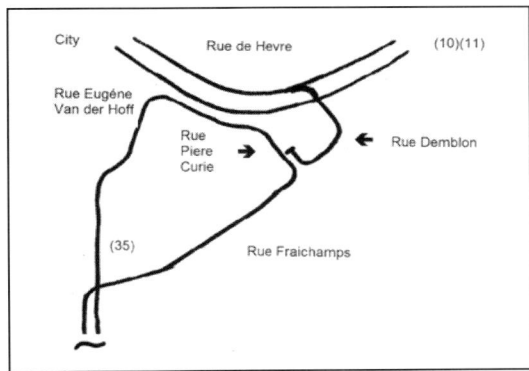

ROBERMONT Terminus did not physically link to 10/11 wires on Rue de Hevre

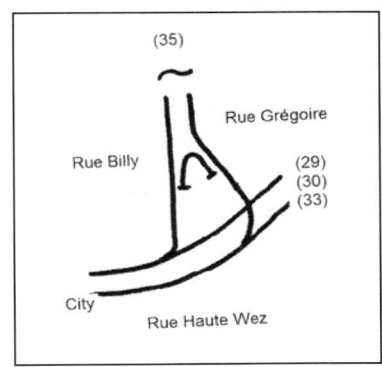

Junction of 35 Robermont from Rue Haute Wez (routes 29/30/33)

The shared routes were mostly to the South and East. Junctions on these are shown with route numbers to indicate the flow of vehicles. Key street names are shown. Perhaps needless-to-say, the diagrams are not to scale!

506 runs round the Robermont loop, adjacent but not connected to the Fleron wires

STREUPAS

With the closure of Streupas (Angleur) trolleybus routes, the junction at Rue Vaudrée became a short-working loop. By 1965 all 26/28 wiring had been removed, from here, and from Quai des Grosses Battes, through to Streupas. 25 Ougrée Beau Site had been diverted via Rue Renory long before, and its junction at Kinkempois removed.

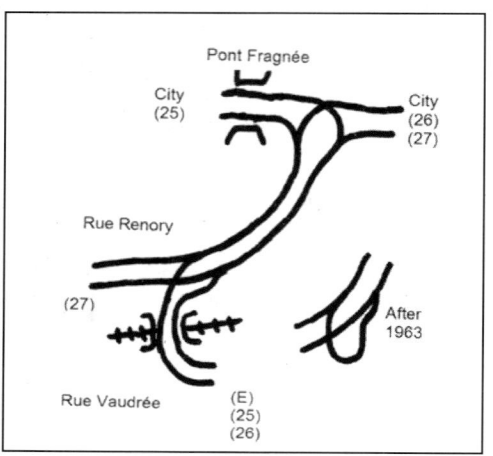

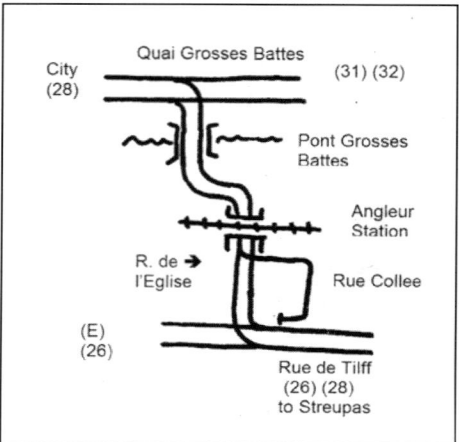

With the advent of one man operation, any facing frogs had to be electrically operated, or the frog removed and wiring designed for the transfer of booms. The electrofrog system was from De La Croix, using two solenoids mounted on the unit, rather than one on a pole at the side like the British system. The triggering contact was mounted about 1m before the frog.

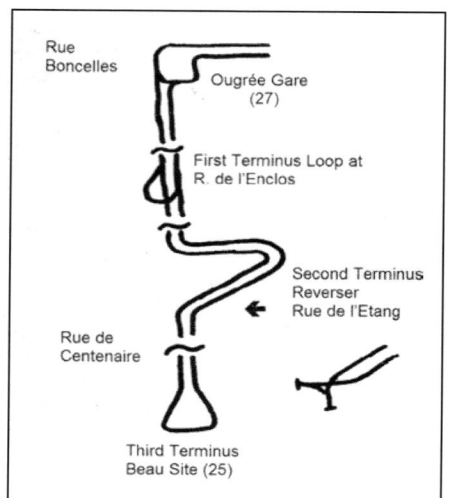

OUGRÉE

The first Ougrée terminus was a loop at Rue de l'Etang, by the municipal cemetery (Beau Site). Latterly the route was extended to the military cemetery (Beau Site) at the junction with Allée de Beau Vivier, and the reverser was removed. The regular turn from Rue Boncelles (adjacent to the LS tram terminus at Ougrée Gare) was introduced when the Renory route was extended to there. When this ended in 1961, the two frogs were removed but turning by depoling remained an option.

Two views of 419 on test with 408 in service on route 20, in 1932.   L

Brossel 499 poses at Ougrée (Beau Site) in 1951 B

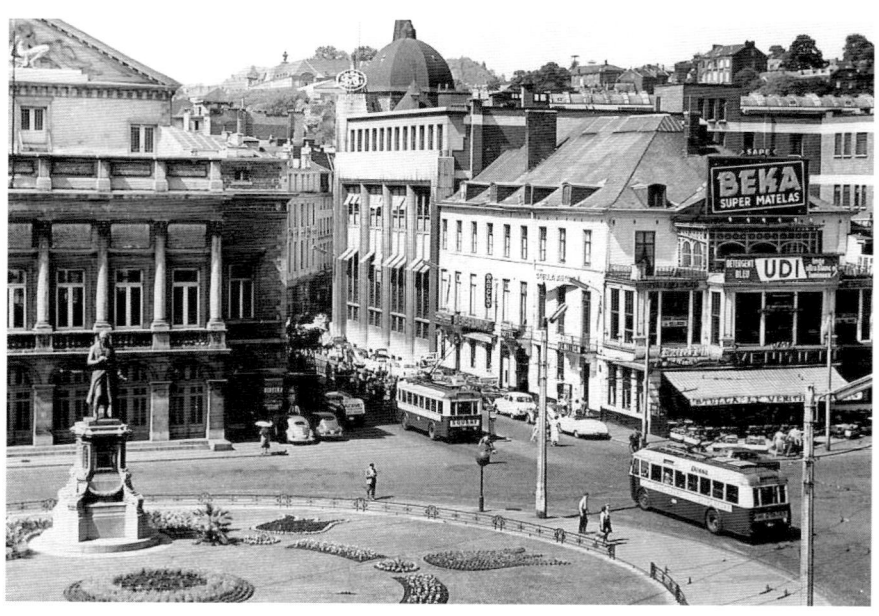

Brossel 499 follows T32 432 out of Pl. de la République Francais, both on service 33

A rebuilt Guillemins 1962. Tram 82 of 1929 on 4 Circular shares the same platforms with Mercedes/Jonckheere 75 of 1954 on ex-trolleybus route 30 Embourg. Trams can still turn at Guillemins but trolleybuses (route 25 remains) only pass through, via Rue Paradis.

Guillemins 1949. Sharing the loading platforms are tram 80 on 4 Circular, a T36 and T32 432 on 24 Thier à Liège which had its terminus at Guillemins at this time.

The TULE Trolleybus Fleet

Year Supplied	Fleet Numbers	Total	Make	Motor hp	Seats	Brakes	Refs
1930	401-405	5	Ransomes	60	26	RM	1
1931	406	1	Ransomes	2 x 40	27	RMa	2
1932/33	407-436	30	FN-CEB	60	26	RGM	3
1936/37	437-484	48	FN-CEB	75	26	RGM	4
1938	485-494	10	FN-CEB	75	26	RGMs	5
1938	495-500	6	Brossel-CEB	75	27	RGMs	6
1939/40	501-518	18	FN-CEB	75	26	RGMs	7
1948	519	1	FN-ACEC	140	30	RA	8
1954/6	520-549	30	FN-ACEC	140	37	RA	9
1957	550	1	FN-ACEC	140	30	RA	10

Refs

1. 2 pedal control. Re-built at least 3 times. The fleet number style changed by 1933. Supplied without retrievers, but with hooks on the near-side of the roof to carry a bamboo. Retrievers were first fitted below the bottom of the rear panel. The front was re-built first with headlights below the access doors, and later mounted on them. The single rear door was at the top of the steps opening outward; the front door was a single fold with a slit to clear the first step when open. The original doors were manual operation, pneumatic when remodelled in 1949, and both doors were changed to two jacknife. Scrapped 1960/61, although 404 survived as a staff 'canteen' at Ste Foy until the late 1960's.

2. 2 pedal control. Considerably re-built. In 1949 a new front was fashioned, featuring high sited headlamps; part fairings over the rear wheels; and conventional trolleys. Scrapped 1961.

3. 3 pedal control. Re-built several times. Original rear door as 1930 Ransomes, with a matching front door. Converted as per Ransomes conversions. Original seating was 30, being a rear nearside bench for 5, and a double forward facing replaced by the conductor's seat. Fitted with Ransomes patent spreader trolley base. An undated works drawing shows: A spare wheel mounted under the rear platform, with a floor hatch to access the lowering mechanism; The only rear light is a single red mounted on the nearside roof corner; There is a rear route number box but no destination box. Designated type T32, the last examples were withdrawn from service in late 1965.

4. 3 pedal control. Similar to T32 but minus the 'bonnet' projection at the front. Side-by-side conventional trolleys. Designated type T36.
5. Similar to T36 but with improved control gear. Designated type T38.
6. 3 pedal control. Intended for 39 standee rather than the usual 30. Built by consortium Brossel-D'Heure-CEB. The last was scrapped in 1961.
7. Another batch of T38. The last of the T36/T38 vehicles was withdrawn on 4 April 1969.
8. Prototype 'large capacity' vehicle. 2 pedal control, with a cam-control system. Top speed of almost 50 mph! It ran in service for 4 years, covering around 200,000 km, but was considered by staff to be 'not up to scratch' mechanically. Said to have been scrapped because of a failed back axle in 1953, its ghost appeared in 1957.
9. 2 pedal control on right foot, with the accelerator on the right. Built under licence from Marmon-Herrington-Westinghouse, the Belgian model was about 1½ tons heavier than the original. Control equipment access through rear doors. Resistances in a protective sleeve under the vehicle, with forced-air cooling (which provided interior heating). 14-step automatic acceleration. Designated type IV.
10. Almost identical to the 1948 model. Differences include: A slightly remodelled front, with rounded corners to the destination box, a more inward sloping windscreen, and headlamps mounted slightly higher. And normal doors – on the '48 model the doors seem to incorporate some sort of drop flap. Designated type VB. It was originally green lower/cream upper. Re-painted in Type IV style in 1962.

When front fenders were fitted, headlights were moved on to the doors. The legend carried by trolleys and motorbuses on the rear fender – "Je roule sur Engelbert" – refers to the tyres. Engelbert had a factory at Longdoz, Liège.

A very comprehensive product description of types IV and VB was published by FN in the late 1950's – in English!

Abbreviations:
FN = Fabrique Nationale d'Armes de Guerre s.a. of Herstal, Liège
CEB = Constructions Electriques de Belgique, of Herstal, Liège
ACEC = Ateliers de Constructions Electriques de Charleroi, Bruxelles.

Brakes
R - Rheostatic   M - Mechanical
G - Regenerative   Ma - Air Assisted
A - Air   Ms - Servo Assisted

5 VOITURES. *1930*. CONSTRUCTION RANSOMES.

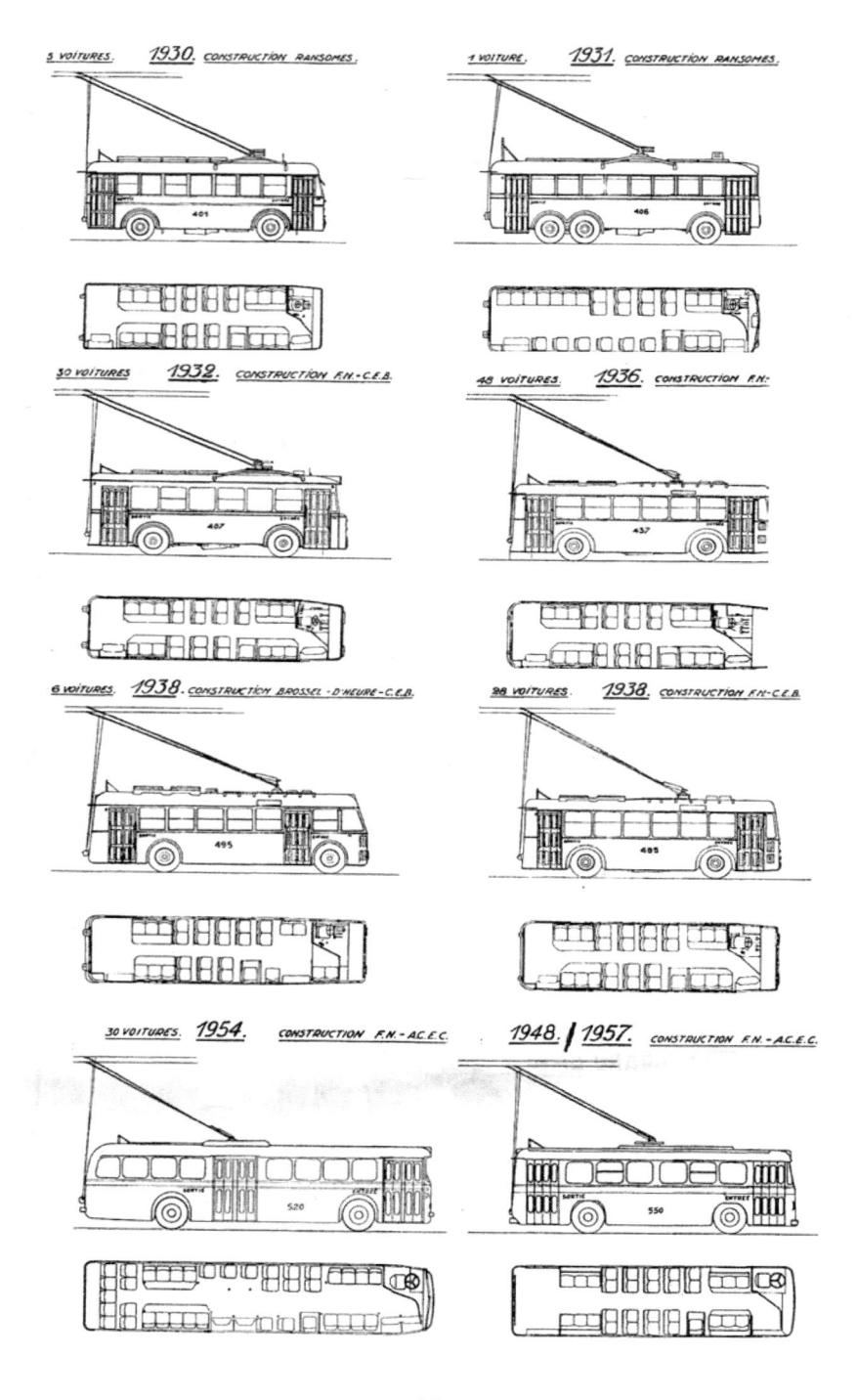

1 VOITURE. *1931*. CONSTRUCTION RANSOMES.

30 VOITURES. *1932*. CONSTRUCTION F.N.-C.E.B.

48 VOITURES. *1936*. CONSTRUCTION F.N.

6 VOITURES. *1938*. CONSTRUCTION BROSSEL-D'HEURE-C.E.B.

38 VOITURES. *1938*. CONSTRUCTION F.N.-C.E.B.

30 VOITURES. *1954*. CONSTRUCTION F.N.-A.C.E.C.

1948 / *1957*. CONSTRUCTION F.N.-A.C.E.C.

404 and 401 at Cointe 1933   B

404 as remodelled in 1949   A

Ransomes catalogue photo of Liège 406.   K

Ransomes 406 as rebuilt in 1949.   A

T32 409, FN catalogue illustration and showing the metal body framework

Two thirds of the T32 fleet posed in Cornillon yard in Winter 1935/6. 425 is ninth from the left. L

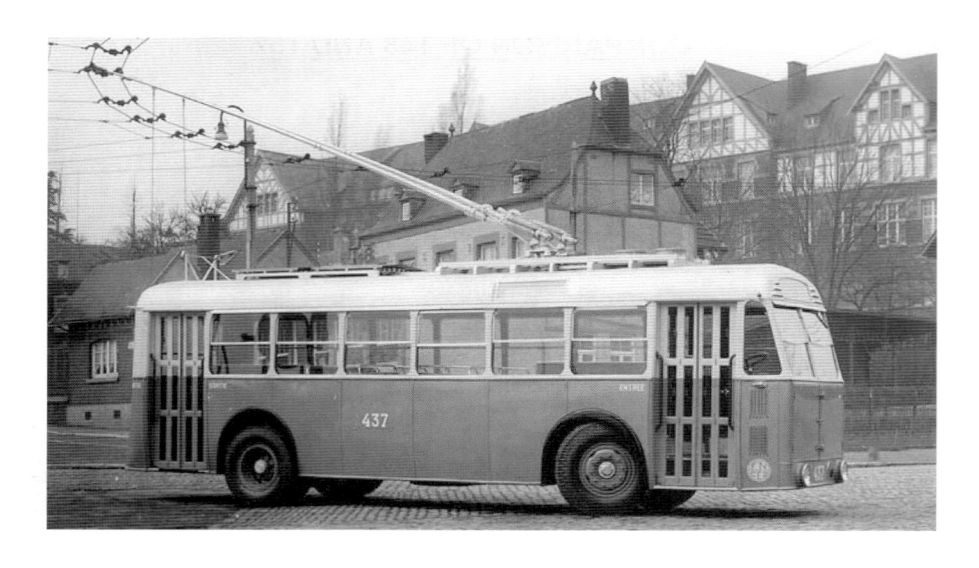

The first T36 No. 437 on test at Cointe.   L

419 alone at Cointe terminus 1932   L

COMPARISON OF T48 AND T57

FN 1948 prototype 519 (although it displays no number) at Pont Fragnée in 1951.   B

Type VB No. 550 at the FN works 1957   L

550 was in green lower/cream upper ex works. Type IV's were silver-grey with a blue band. Around 1962 all were repainted silver-grey with a green band, as was 550, seen here in Cornillon yard.

Comparison of fronts, 550 and Type IV No. 525   1966

ERRATA
The Gremlins have accessed two pages!

Page 32
- Diagram top left, and text: The loop shown "after 1963" is pure fiction - It became plain wire.
- Top diagrams: (E) denotes these routes join together.
- Lower text: "The first Ougrée terminus was at Rue de l'Enclos ……" as on the diagram.

Page 45   Captions should read:

Top: T36 456 for Ougrée and TULE Tram 178 on 4 (Circular) at the SNCB railway crossing in rue de Sclessin. The tail of wiring from rue Bovy can be seen on the left. The rail link was to the customs house on rue Paradis – an SNCB employee is rolling back the barrier for 456 to proceed.

Lower: After the morning peak, 487 chases 509 back to Cornillon depot.

T36 456 from Ougrée and TULE Tram 178 on 4 (circular) at the end of Rue de Fétinne, crossing the Trooz tramlines in Rue des Vennes in 1959. The tail of the school loop via Rue de Vergers can be seen on the left.   B

487 chases 509 along Rue Bidout.   D

501 turns from the St Walburge route at R. du Gen. Bertrand, heading for Burenville. D

489 leaves Burenville. D

Repaints from the early 1960's were silver-grey with a green waistband. 485 near Pl. Jules Seeliger en route from St. Walburge   D

The standard Liège livery was blue lower, cream upper, grey roof. 515 circumnavigates Pl. J. Seeliger, en route from St. Walburge   D

471 at Chevremont terminus, now just a loop with a trailing frog of the former 32

471 bound for Chevremont, squeezes under the railway bridge at Rue de la Station

531 meets tram 71 at Pl. Coronmeuse in 1960   B

FN/ACEC Type IV No. 520 at Oupeye terminus   L

Chaos. 532 doesn't quite fit between the motorbuses cluttering Pl. St. Lambert

Calm. 485 climbs Bvd. Cesar Thomson en route to St. Walburge. D

545 follows 526 into ANS LONCIN terminus

532 enters Pl. St Lambert, over the dual-gauge TULE/SNCV tramlines, 1967

531 crosses the Pont d'Amercoeur, en route for Fleron

548 turns at Beyne 1968

RAILWAYS ECONOMIQUES DE LIÈGE-SERAING

Commencing in 1882, the company operated metre-gauge steam trams from Jemeppe church via Tilleur to Liège, with a depot at Sclessin near Pont d'Ougrée. The fleet was 14 locomotives, numbered 1-12, 14, 15 to avoid 'unlucky' 13. Three years later the line was converted to standard gauge, and penetrated further into Liège. In 1904 the line was electrified and finally reached Liège Théâtre. Meanwhile in 1900 a second metre gauge line was built from Seraing Pont to Seraing Lize (Place du Poiray) on the south side of the Meuse. This was electrified from the outset. Soon a new bridge was built over the Meuse at Seraing; the second line was converted to standard gauge, and the two lines were linked. A new depot was constructed on Rue Gustave Baivy at Jemeppe. The northern line was extended to Flémalle Haute, the southern line to Biens Communaux (Rue de Pleinevaux).

A disconnected spur was laid from the RELSE tramline at Sclessin, down Avenue E. Vandervelde, over the Nouveau Pont d'Ougrée, along Quai Louva and R. Jos. Wauters to Ougrée station. This lasted for one week – a tram from Ougrée Gare failed to turn on to Quai Louva, missed the old Pont d'Ougrée and plunged into the river! The Schlessin-Ougrée Gare shuttle was maintained by a RELSE motorbus service until the destruction of the bridges in 1940. In 1941 the old Pont d'Ougrée was reinstated, and a tramline laid from a triangular junction on the Liège-Jemeppe line, along Rue Malvoz, Rue J. Wauters to meet the TULE trolleybus route at Ougrée Gare.

Although we are primarily concerned with trolleybuses, mention must be made here of one of many unusual features of the RELSE system – the amphibian tram or 'tram canard'. This was No. 51, a short wheelbase open side crossbench car, with the motor and electrics mounted centrally above the floor. The idea was that, with the periodic flooding of the Meuse, this tram could cope with about 60cm of flood water. If the electrics got wet, the passengers were already in it 'up to their ankles'! The vehicle is shown paired with a similar trailer and appears to be equipped for push-pull working.

In 1932 consideration was given to a trolleybus line along the south bank from Marihaye (Rue du Many, west of Banque) via Yvoz to Ramet, but the necessary formalities proceeded at snail pace. Instead the first trolleybus route opened in 1936 and was from Châtqueue via Rue de Papillon to Seraing Banque – well, almost! The desired terminus at Châtqueue was at a small square, with no space for a turning circle. Worse still, a railway level crossing was situated immediately south of Banque, and the RELSE were not allowed to put wires over the railway. Again there was no room for a turning circle. Rather than make concessions to the route – for example using the tram overbridge nearby at Seraing, and extending the line to a more open area beyond Châtqueue – the RELSE had the firm of Brossel design a double-ended trolleybus! The route was wired with conventional both directions overhead but terminated as stub ends. There were no frogs.

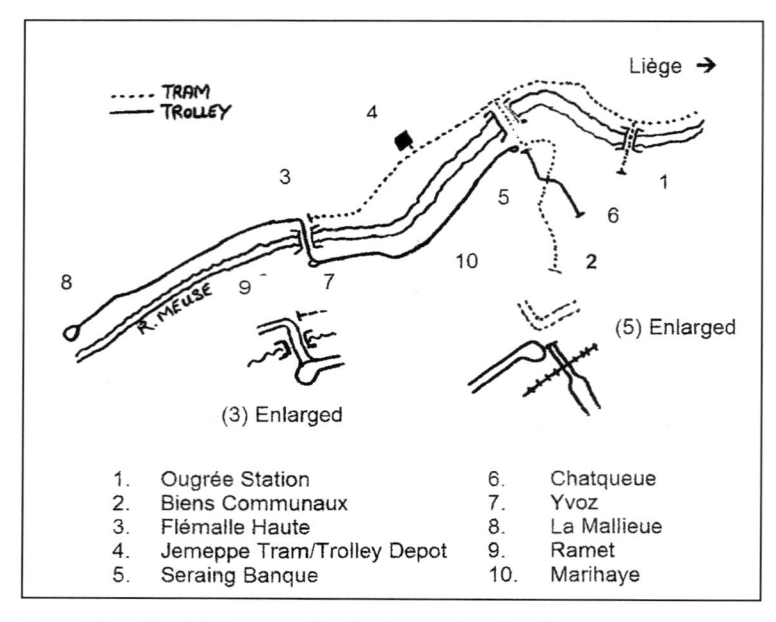

1. Ougrée Station
2. Biens Communaux
3. Flémalle Haute
4. Jemeppe Tram/Trolley Depot
5. Seraing Banque
6. Chatqueue
7. Yvoz
8. La Mallieue
9. Ramet
10. Marihaye

General plan of the RELSE tram and trolleybus network. The tram route to Ougrée Station met the TULE trolleybus routes 25 and 27 there.

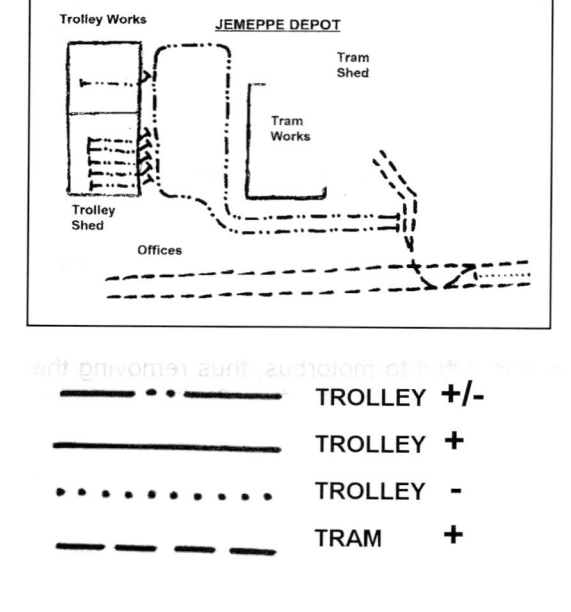

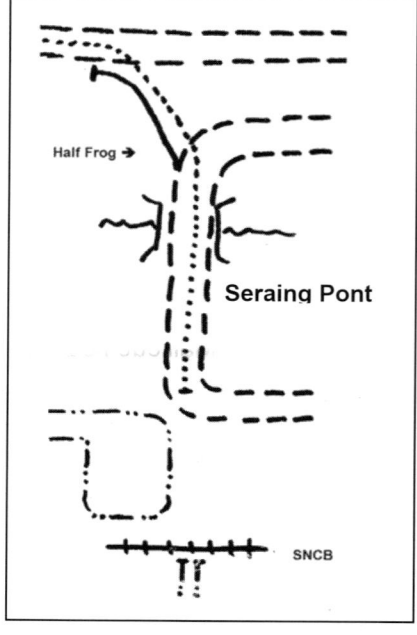

TROLLEY +/-
TROLLEY +
TROLLEY -
TRAM +

In 1938 the route along the river opened, from Seraing Banque just over the level crossing from the other route, and out to Yvoz. Four more double-ended vehicles were ordered for this route.

Together with other bridges along the Meuse, the Pont de Seraing was destroyed in 1940. On the morning after the destruction, and subsequently as necessary, trolleybuses were towed from Jemeppe depot to Liège, taken by barge across the Meuse, then towed to Seraing Banque. A garage on Rue Francisco Ferrer was used to shed two trolleybuses overnight, traction batteries being used for access. In 1941 the Pont d'Ougrée was reconstructed enabling towing over the river at that point.

In 1942 a trolleybus line was opened along the north side of the river, from Flémalle Haute tram terminus to Engis. Again this had no turning loops, but was double line throughout. A railway crossing separated the tram and trolley lines at Flémalle Haute. As at Seraing, all vehicles used traction batteries to cross the railway, then tram overhead plus a skate to travel to and from Jemeppe depot. As a concession, some trolley wiring was erected in the depot yard, and later a centrally placed negative wire from near to the yard (but not into it) along the tram route to just before Seraing bridge. You can imagine the poling/depoling required from trolleybus shed to the Châtqueue route! A short length of trolley overhead enabled connection between the two tram routes at Seraing bridge.

When the SNCB took over railway operation, two pairs of trolleybus wires were permitted over the Seraing crossing, close together to clear the lifting barriers. These were not connected to the other route, and were to facilitate depot journeys only.

About this time a turning loop was provided via Rue Goffant/Rue de la Station at Banque and another at Yvoz directly across the river from Flémalle Haute. To operate this service two conventional 6-wheel trolleys were purchased.

In 1943 the north bank route reached La Mallieue.

In 1948, the two river routes were joined with a new bridge at Flémalle Haute. The turning loop at Yvoz remained, boasting the only electric frog on the system; and La Mallieue had a turning loop.

In 1949 the Châtqueue route was converted to motorbus, thus removing the requirement for double ended vehicles. Of the six, the four 6-wheelers were converted to single-ended, the two 4-wheelers were scrapped.

In 1951, two conventional Brossel 4-wheel vehicles were purchased, but by 1961, the trolleybus fleet was down to 4.

There was a 30 minute headway for Seraing to La Mallieue (about 12 km), with a Seraing-Yvoz in between, requiring 3 vehicles.

All trolleybus operations ceased 30/8/63. The Liège-Jemeppe Pont tram closed 30/11/67, and final abandonment was 30/4/68.

The RELSE Trolleybus Fleet

A purchasing company called Electrorail supplied RELSE trolleybuses, new or second-hand.

401/402: Designed by Brossel frères, Bovy et Pipe in 1935, these were 3-axle vehicles, with a 3-pedal driving position at each end. The double wheeled centre axle was driven by two 52 hp motors from ACEC. The two end axles steered simultaneously. There were two pairs of conventional trolleys, with fixed retrievers. Hydraulic brakes operated on the steering wheels, with a parking brake on the motor drive shafts. Double jacknife doors were fitted at each end opposite the driver (who also had a cab door). With 28 seats plus 32 standees, they were just over 10 metres long and just over 10 tons weight empty. As with the later double ended vehicles they had traction batteries of limited capacity – a range of 50 metres or more! Enough to get over the level crossing or across the road at the depot. One vehicle was exhibited at the 1935 Brussels Exhibition, on the Electrorail stand.

403/404: The same model as 401/402. Supplied in 1937.

402 and 502 both in original form, and seen at Banque on the Châtqueue route   A

501/502: Diminutive 4-wheel double ended, designed by Brossel, supplied in 1937. These were to replace 401/402 on the Châtqueue route. Both axles steered, and they had one 52 hp motor. They were 7.64m long, seating 17 with 10 standees, and weighing around 6 tons empty. Opposite each driving position was a three-part folding door – the left part folded inwards, the double right part jacknifed – and, of course, there was a cab door! Trolleys were of the one-above-the-other type so they could be turned end-to-end. Retrievers were not fitted – just a couple of lengths of rope! The RELSE considered them "extremely manoeuvrable". Another reference to these vehicles states: Motor 60 hp, and fitted with retrievers.

Jemeppe depot, with 502, and 404 (in rebuilt form)   B

Guy EB701 (RELSE 601), as shown at the Liège Exhibition 1930   N

601/602: Built in 1929 for the SNCV, these were 3-axle Guy vehicles, with 37 seat, recessed centre entrance English bodywork. One was exhibited at the 1930 Liège Exhibition. Painted in dark brown and cream livery, they were numbered EB701/EB702. The SNCV line from Etterbeek to Overijse was not constructed and the vehicles were stored at Overijse depot, being used as sheds for breeding rabbits! They were purchased by RELSE in 1942, who considerably rebuilt them including an extra doorway at the back, and gave them the numbers 601/602, and the RELSE livery of two-tone green with a dark red waistband.

701/702: Two conventional 4-wheel Brossel/ACEC vehicles. Built in 1946 for the SNCV (the Overijse line again?) the order was cancelled, and they were stored until purchased by the RELSE in 1951, presumably to replace the two Guys. 601/602 and 701/702 did not have traction batteries.

Brossel 701 in RELSE livery, prior to commencing public service, on the La Mallieue route, 1951.   B

403 has just left the terminus at Seraing, en route for Ivoz.   Taken in 1949   B

403 at Yvoz terminus 1950   B

JEMEPPE DEPOT – The Trolleybus Yard, with the tram depot and works in the background

*401 and 402 in final form.
With only one route, destination blinds were unnecessary   B*

Guy 602, as rebuilt by RELSE. The destination blind shows ENGIS   B

THE ACCUBUSES

These were battery vehicles, purchase by the Exhibition organisers to provide transport between the two parts of the Liège Exhibition of 1930. The route, all on the East side of the Meuse, was Place d'Italie, Rue Leon Frédérica, Rue Méean, Place Delcour, Rue Louis Jamme, Place d'Amercoeur, Quai Bonaparte, Avenue Georges Truffaut and to the South end of Pont de l'Atlas.

Originally 4 vehicles were ordered from Société Belge de Traction Electrique par Accumulateurs (SBTEA) of Brussels. The chassis was from Miesse; Body by Jonckheere; Electric folding doors, motors and control equipment by ACEC. By way of assessment, each vehicle had a different battery set: Edison 300 A/h, Tudor 400 A/h, Kathanode (GB) 320 A/h. The fourth would have been Saift, but before it was completed, three vehicles were deemed sufficient.

Each vehicle had two 24 hp motors (160v, 900 rpm) fixed outside the chassis driving the rear wheels through shafts. There were 4 crates of batteries, each of 21 lead-acid or 36 nickel-iron cells. There was 2-pedal control, with rheostatic and dual mechanical brakes.

The vehicle wheelbase was 17 feet; the body had a wooden frame and roof, with aluminium sides. There were 32 seats with 18 standees. The turning circle was about 52 feet. With a full load, the net weight was around 12.5 tons.

It was envisaged that the batteries would provide 50 miles of running per charge, with a top speed (fully laden) of 23 mph. In practice, recharging took place after about 43 miles. The top speed was around 22 mph, with a creditable average service speed of over 13 mph. The journey time was about 7 minutes.

Accubus No. 3 in service in Liège 1930   A

After the exhibition they were stored in the yard at the Cornillon depot, though the TULE did not own them. In 1940, one was scrapped; one was bought by a factory in Grivegnée, Liège where it was converted into a battery powered flat wagon; the third retained its body, had ex-tram trolleys fitted, and had tanks for the transportation of gas fixed inside. By night, it traversed the Ougrée route to a gas producer (Usine de l'Azote) to bring gas to Natalis depot for use in TULE tower wagons. Trolleybus wiring was erected along Rue R. Heinz and into the right hand shed road, especially for this vehicle. The vehicle was given TULE fleet number 20, and on the rear was painted 'Défense d'approcher avec du feu' (no naked lights). After the War, both vehicles were scrapped.

Natalis depot 1943. The gas transporter ex Accubus is in the right hand shed road   B

Grease Wagon

Because Liège used carbon-less trolley heads, which created considerable wear on the overhead, a tower wagon was fitted with two trolleys on the tower. The trolley head was simply a guide, and fixed immediately behind it was a grease tank with a roller applicator and a fixed brush, in contact with the wires. The grease wagon toured the routes after every 3500 to 4000 trolleybus passes.

THE DEWANDRE TROLLEYBUS

This vehicle was built around 1934 by inventor Albert Dewandre of Liège.

It was extremely innovative in that it was front-wheel drive, with a 65 hp motor mounted over the front axle driving through worm, differential and cardan shafts. Access to the motor was by a hinged panel on the front of the vehicle. The driver's seat was arranged high, to clear the motor and also the transverse inverted leaf spring which passed over the motor and provided much of the front wheel suspension. The chassis was welded frame, carrying a 36 seat/34 standee, 2-door body. The unladen weight was 11 tons. Up to the end of February 1936 the vehicle was reported to have travelled about 10,000 miles in service, with no problems. It ran for about two years on the Liège network.

One intention of front wheel drive was to provide a lower saloon floor to enable quicker loading and unloading. Against this was poor use of space – in front of the front door was taken up with motor, controls and suspension.

Photos show the vehicle in two guises, with completely different front ends. Possibly the bodywork was altered before entering service in Liège since an article by M. Harmel, Directeur General of TULE, and dated June 1935, shows the modified front end, as seen below.

ODDITIES

The silver trolleybus was a French-built vehicle brought to Liège in late 1931 or early 1932 for test purposes, as France had no trolleybus route at the time. It was destined for Casablanca. It was given the temporary fleet number 407, indicating the date was after delivery of Ransomes 406 but before FN407. It is seen here at Cointe. It has just driven over tramlines, a remnant of the Tramway de Cointe, taken over by the RELSE in 1905, and later abandoned.   B

In 1958 the SNCV experimented to see if, in the event of a prolonged fuel crisis, it would be feasible to convert diesel buses to trolleybuses. (The question of erecting overhead does not seem to have been addressed!) Electrics were provided by ACEC, and the vehicle, seen here at Pl. St Lambert, was successfully tested in service for about 3 months, carrying the registration 0717.P.
It was then reconverted to diesel.   N